THE SELF CONQUERING BATTALION.......

THE DANCERS WHO STARTED DANCING WITHIN!!!

JULIET K. MONDOL

ISBN 978-1-68509-040-1

I sincerely dedicate this story to all the women who would like to think beyond themselves. This story is a reflection of what goes on within a woman and how she looks forward to a person who can make changes to her life. This person can be just the next-door neighbor....or even an acquaintance who would become a dear friend for the much-needed change. There are a lot of things that go within our hearts. We just need to feel it and try for ways to come in connection with it and thus grow.

Contents

Foreword

This is to thank all those women who would expand beyond themselves. I thank my dear friends who gave me the belief and confidence that they will be going ahead with this and staying with me till the end. My friends loved it as they felt it was so real. They enjoyed reading the manuscript not because they were a part of it but because they felt the whole scene was moving before their eyes. A big thanks to Mrs. Nayar who read it and felt really emotional. She started crying because she felt that her inner, deep emotions were now being understood. My friend Mita felt that she has now found a true friend and my friend Rachita now feels that taking out time for herself is worth it. A big thank you to all the ladies who trusted me for what I can do, who thought I can help them change their ways of thinking and thus growing. I was overjoyed to see the change.

Preface

Enter Caption

"Let not limits define you, instead be the definition of your evolving limits"

I am a psychologist by profession. I am very happy to be in this profession. The reason is that not only this profession has made immense changes in my viewpoint towards people but it has tremendously increased my observation skills. Now after practicing for more than thirteen years and planning to go on, as an 'Evolved Psychologist", I feel that people in today's quick world need easy, handy, and practical solutions to the problems of everyday life that might seem like a "mountain despite being a mole". For this, it is very important to think about the patient as myself and what kind of help I would have liked from a practitioner? I need to put myself in a position of the patient to be able to solve problems.

My applied psychology, mindfulness, counseling, and behavior analysis from India and abroad have helped me grow within myself. It has helped me to evolve and know myself better. This part of me, this evolution is very important because only if you know yourself better can you help others effectively. It is only then you know the areas you can work properly and the areas that might cause you to underperform. As I would like to be of great help to the people who seek help from me, I would happily consider two things to be effective. Firstly whether the given task exactly defines my boundary of working and secondly how honest can I be first with myself and then with the patient? This will help me in building a trusting therapeutic alliance with the patient. I am glad that I could achieve this through my career and am therefore able to take it forward through my creative skills like dancing and writing during the Pandemic, where I hope to make some difference in people's lives with all my learning and skills. This Pandemic has taught me not to waste what you have as this skill of yours may become a life-changer for many.

Acknowledgements

Acknowledgment

This work would not have been possible without my friends who have been a motivating part of this whole journey.

The role of their families in supporting them through this novel venture is highly appreciated.

It felt good when their children took their videos and sent them to me for corrections. In a way, we all got very engaged. At least there was something else that we all looked forward to and that was rebuilding hope and companionship.

My deepest thanks to the families of Mr. Kopadda, Mr. Patle, Mr. Das and Mr. Mondol.

As this story is based upon true events, there was no intention to hurt each other's feelings but the only purpose was to develop an expansive "SELF"

Prologue

It is always challenging to do something new, something out of the box! Sometimes we don't even know how beautiful an experience can be, even if we do not have any first-hand experience about it. Then experiencing the beauty of something not witnessed before exposes us to the subtle emotions not attended to earlier.

My dear friends residing in the same colony as I do take up the challenge of learning dancing on the virtual model. They decided to do this class to beat the boredom of the same everyday household routine that included cooking, cleaning, and taking care of the family, at times even becoming grumpy with the lined-up household chores. So this for some was becoming too much to handle. They realized that they were becoming irritable and were shouting at kids, sometimes even when things could be easily handled if given a thought.

To keep up my dancing passion and learning, I used to do some small functions apart from my professional commitments as a psychologist. The interesting part was that my friends wanted to learn from me. As I have been trained in Indian classical dance, Kathak, from Bhatkhande, I surely was very much loved among my friends. For my friends, it was a challenge because no one was a trained dancer, though they aspired to be one during their childhood. They were cornered by the dictates of conventions that forced them to learn cooking and do the bare minimum of education. My friends with all their problems and taboos decided to now break free!

To their surprise, they witnessed a whole new world of their own. They discovered an online world that was not judgemental and evaluative. This world just tried to bring out the best in each other. My friends started becoming more technology savvy, they started talking in terms related to the "e-world" which in itself was great learning. We were learning again! We were now learning to live our childhood dreams which had somehow got lost in the roles we played as a mother, wife, sister, daughter, and many societal connections which at times were happily bestowed, without consideration, of course! My friends now thought that not knowing whether they have played their roles well or not, as there will remain an objective probability of error, they took upon the activity of being an "admirer of self". So, my lovely friends decided to dance to their inner tunes. We were not only learning dancing and its nuances that keep on evolving with time but also a subtle way to love ourselves, nurture ourselves, and therefore make the environment around us much happier.

People might term it as being selfish, but this selfishness was different from the one where we are totally not worried about others being and only think of our gains. This selfishness was divine. I will tell you why. My friends after a whole day's work made it a point to keep aside some time for themselves, to love doing what they once dreamt of, and above all did not blame anyone for the lost time of self-nurturance. This selfishness came with layers of goodness that showcased itself in different ways. It showed that if my friends were happy with themselves, they will not only spread love and compassion but would also stop blaming others for their faults. This selfishness taught them to smile at mistakes and reform them without a hitch. If it was possible with "self" then making a change was never difficult. They now were more accepting and loving of their family's mistakes. They had now learned the art of not being irritable because that caused more harm than happiness by being understanding of other's limits. We all had expanded within ourselves. We have made space inside us to accept, understand, move on and dance with what is uncertain. We were positively selfish.....yes we love ourselves because we love you!

CHAPTER ONE

THE SELF CONQUERING BATTALION......

The Dancers who Started Dancing Within!!!

By
Juliet Karmakar Mondol
Counsellor
Indian Institute of Technology
Kharagpur.

Every Saturday evening, the phone was supposed to be handy....the reason was obvious, sending a WhatsApp message to join "The Dance Class"! Why I call it "obvious" is because, during the Pandemic, 2020, the phone with its various Intra and inter functions was the only way to communicate. It slowly became the source of all activities, be it news, webinars, classes, shopping, booking, banking which till the time the Pandemic broke out did not find much footage. The Pandemic made phones a necessity. My group of battalions used this facility to come out of the cocoon to which they were conventionally inclined.

My battalion was not trained, neither were they going to attend a class that follows rules, what it followed was respect for untrained dancers, love for their humility, and salute to their sincerity. It was surprising to see that a little bit of encouragement and help made them develop some skills that they might not have been born with but had the inner longing to do one day or the other. The only connecting medium....a smartphone, in whatever capacity it may have been. The battalion comprises a group of ladies from diverse cultures, places, and languages. These ladies were comprised of strength that necessitated more learning, took their faults laughingly that left me with unimaginable enthusiasm to teach them in the best possible manner. The battalion was not formed with much thought. It just came out of a group thought which started with some ladies in my colony coming together to form a group. The name of the group was Women Unshackeling. The purpose of this was to unshackle oneself from the household chores for some time and try and be loving towards self by participating in some activities that we thought of carrying out every month. It was a way of connecting with laughter, joy, cuisines, mirth, togetherness amidst diversity, and various degrees of pain and sorrow in a more adaptive way.

One Friday evening, the phone rings. Tired from work, thinking that it would be another obligatory call, I started searching around for my phone in the darkness of my bag, as I returned home from work only at that time. Believe me, the strength of answering the phone was dwindling. With fear of what my office would ask me to do something unwanted on the weekend, tried to disconnect my ringing phone....." Oh!!!! Stop, stop...It is Mrs. Nayar, just two buildings away from my house. "Maybe an invite for some south Indian delicacies over the weekend" was the immediate thought that came to my mind. With all these words doing a to and fro in my head.....were indeed responsible for my delayed reaction. I rang her back. Mrs. Nayar immediately picked up the phone....She said

"Hello, madam....are you busy?"

"No Mrs. Nayar..absolutely not"...just waiting for the invitation to come through!

Mrs. Nayar -" Madam..we will keep a meeting of only ladies tomorrow at 8:00 PM. Please come"

My desire to have the delicious dosas that Mrs. Nayar has been feeding us grew even stronger. My taste buds and mind could not be in sync and so I uttered...

"Mrs. Nayar... of course I will come. But what about snacks? Would you like me to get some from the reliable sweet shop?"

My expectation of Mrs. Nayar saying "NO" and offering some homemade dosas was overruled. My dosas were no more being prepared for the meeting and so sadly enough I was getting some snacks from the market!!!

Very much enthusiastic about the meeting barring my dosa expectation, all the ladies from the colony gathered at Mrs. Nayar's house. Some had just taken their vaccines, so many arguments were happening for and against the vaccine. For myself not interested in doing any debate in the weekend, I wanted something lighter to be discussed. So with some senior ladies of the colony, we decided to have a group on the wats app. It was called "Women Unshackling" where we can all share our talents in some form or the other. Realizing that my dosas would not happen again in the short run, I was constantly thinking of some excuse that could get me to Mrs. Nayar's house and her delicious dosas. The group was formed. The opening of the group, though virtual had a physical opening.

"Mrs. Das's son got a job". Mrs. Das was a saree lover...and kept herself busy with not only office work but also buying sarees. She would drape a saree in five minutes...her swiftness was adorable. A Bengali woman with a fondness for sarees was the first person in the group to initiate a group activity that was "dining out". It all started with her son getting a job....Thinking on the hind side..how did that matter to us...but really may be longing for social togetherness was something that brought us close. Something different from our monotonous daily routine! A piece of news that spread in the group.....in a form that was not quite "Chinese whispers". We were all happy...and guess what, my taste buds and mind till now have not settled down, asked Mrs. Das for a treat in a South Indian Hotel. The first visit of the virtual group in the physical world.

Mrs. Das asked..." How will we go?"

"In a Toto" - I answered

Everyone started laughing...... In a Toto....

We need two...said, Mrs. Ghosh, who was constantly worried about her falling hair and gaining waistline. With curly hair...Mrs. Ghosh loved to talk over the phone and didn't quite worry about quickly finishing her work on time.

The Manual Toto....the laughter initiative

"Yes, I think we can manage.....in case of shortage let us squeeze into one another...the lighter ones on top of the heavier ones...."

Smiles started pouring in and everyone started looking at their waistlines....maybe the first time we looked at ourselves and started laughing at our waistlines. A feeling that was not shaming but was accepting "as things were". To us, this was "coming together". If only the world had not shamed us for what we looked like!! The world hardly cares about people being worried about their waistlines that might in itself speak about a lot of complications. The world not understanding its nuances enjoys shaming, a work that does not require much thinking!

Arranging toto could be so much fun and strategic.....something that I got reacquainted with, after my college days. I guess organization has been a skill that needed some identification from my side. Well...this was the time that helped me to look at some things I may have overlooked. The group was helping me to praise myself.....an activity for which we rarely have time.

Finally, the day arrived when my hidden desire to have the dosa at Mrs. Nayar's house was somewhat full by having the dosa at a restaurant. As we entered the restaurant...the waiters seemed delighted...as if we were the people they were waiting for...whom they might have thought will roll off money....Well, we did look like "food lovers"!!!

As one table will not be enough, they happily with enough dexterity, joined the two tables...while we as usual were trying to look for the menu card. If only Mrs. Nayar would have given us a treat our some money would have been saved!!! After having seated in the big chairs...Mrs. Das asked..." Please order. Feel free to order whatever you like....."

Oh...Taste Buds!!!

Having returned from the office we all were very hungry....not able to manage our hunger drive...we had plateful...some even overate. Some had chowmein, idli sambhar and others had Chola bhatura, a fantastic Punjabi masala rich food. Our stomach also looked like the puffed-up bread made with regular all-purpose white flour, oil, soda, and curd after we had a stomach full. My friend Mita...ordered a plate of fish fry. Being an avid lover of fish, Mita did not try to be different! Probably this kept her happy. I on the other hand...tried to have some seafood along with idlis. A rare combination...but that was exciting. Mrs. Gosh being as ever-cheerful...shared some seafood with me...while others enjoyed having their somewhat favorite cuisines, I preferred a creative delight for my otherwise craving and cursing taste buds!! It is always difficult to come out of comfort zones....but at times a try can make the difference. Mrs. Ghosh...with her satiated look asked..." will someone have cold drinks? I need something to digest my food". Thinking of the agony the stomach muscles were going through, I did not quite like the idea. Putting the muscles through a lot of tough physical activity was something that made me feel uncomfortable...but if only Mrs. Ghosh could hear her muscles crying!!

The stomach muscle developing coping skills to fight with masala, coke, and tea

Putting them through the torture she ordered "large Coke". I tried to help my stomach organs to relax by ordering tea. Not that I was considerate...but as it happens in daily life, it becomes much easier to be judgmental of others...but with "self" everything" is just fine!!!.

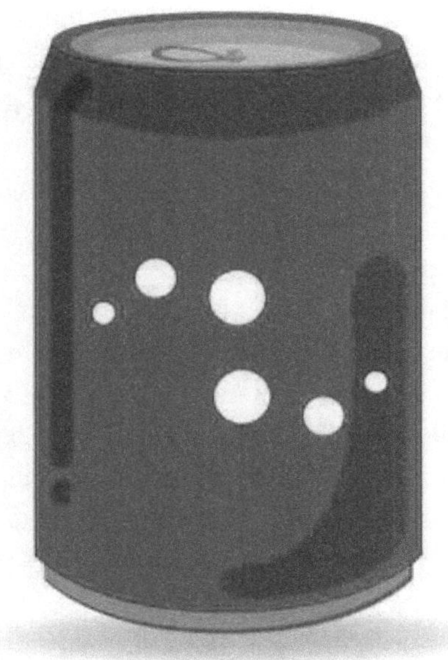

The coke masala fight

Having completed our quota of food....Mrs. Das was ready to pay the bill as it was her grand "forced" treat for us. Having enjoyed ourselves at the restaurant with various delicacies from north Indian to south Indian and also from east to west...little did we realize that we were in our small little way were defining the new meaning of harmonious India. Suddenly my phone rang....oh...no...it was not an official call. Neither was it any friendly call...it was a call from the toto man...he said ...in a loud and defined voice, much of it which they were used to at home, ways in which they were used to talking with the females of the house said....' how long do I need to wait?" For me, not wishing to let go of the "unshackling" procedure, that made everyone laugh and enjoy the evening, I told him..".just wait for another half an hour.....don't worry we will give you extra waiting charge." the loud defined voice changed into the most obedient voice....." OK...I was just asking....please take your time". Money does speak!!

At around 9:00 PM we moved out of the restaurant.....laughing and giggling about things that somehow needed group participation. Sitting in the toto after having our stomachs full, gave us more energy to speak. The toto ride was fun....shouting at each other and overtaking each other's toto, manually gave us enough time to have some mischievous exchange with each other. The security at the entrance saw us but smiled his way through as if allowing the connections to grow unhindered. Mrs. Das was kind enough to pay the overhead charges....we all objected but Mrs. Das's goodness had a carryover effect!!!

I asked my friend..".Mita...when are we meeting next.....?" Unsure of the answer...her eyes and smile reassured me of wanting to meet again soon, but "when" had no answer. Mrs. Nayar....standing down just after getting down from the toto said "why don't we start some activity as a group". Mrs. Das....Shouted ...." wait..let me pay...I will join your conversation." Fiddling around in the purse for some change...that the toto man asked for...Mrs. Das took some time to find the new currency that quite matched her purse. With straining retina and pupil activity, Mrs. Das needed some help with money finding. Being tired with the process the toto man...got more than he was promised. Being delighted about his unexpected income...he said...in a humble and obedient voice..." Call me again...I will surely come." Notwithstanding the probability of a second friendly manual voyage....we said" of course Dada (a word used by Bengalis that shows respect to a senior person)....we will take your number from...Mrs. Roy, The one who called you. We will call you wherever we need or our husbands are not around. With the idea of having got more "sawaris" than imagined the otherwise defined voice with his fellow mate...waved us goodbye and left....hoping for a second call...that would surely compensate him, with more than what the economy demands!!

As always being very social, I said...." yes, of course, Mrs. Nayar..that is wonderful. But what can we do?" Different options came up like starting cooking and having parties on weekends, or some singing nights with only women, or some crafts, stitching, and knitting. Mrs. Nayar was nodding her head to all the options but gazing at me as if she wanted something from me....Looking at her I asked her. Mrs. Nayar..what do you think, what can be good for us?' She answered in a very passive voice.

"Madam..as you dance so well...why don't you teach us dancing?" looking down on the slippers that shone at night...as if she demanded something unacceptable.

My eyes opened as wide as they could! With a sigh, I said...Oh.Mrs. Nayar... are you serious? She said yes of course. With all the options pushed behind curtains ....the group decided that dance will be the activity where group members will learn from me. Acknowledging the fact that no one was a trained dancer, what made me very enthusiastic about the activity was their belief in me and the respect and love they had for my passion. Without letting anyone talk in between...I said 'YES".

As tradition would have its residue.....no good work comes without a bargain. Some members did not quite like

Mrs. Nayar's idea. Mrs. Anita Nayar was broken when someone in the group asked her to do something else because according to their judgment, neither did she have the figure nor the training to dance. The night was having its effects on Mrs. Nayar's thoughts....but thankfully enough...with some stars shining..it was important to see how these small stars illuminated the sky...which without them was dark empty hollow space, totally directionless. I felt bad that the conventional stereotype society that we live in does not intentionally consider the courage that Mrs. Anita showed while asking to do a dance activity. I was appalled at her ability to learn being senior to me which by now, I was confirmed not only in age but also in thoughts and actions. As I could not afford to be rude to other members of the unshackling group who were indirectly again trying to put us in shackles, said in a very assertive voice....."It is OK Mrs. Shah.....let's give it a try.....I am sure Mrs. Nayar will prove otherwise. Why can't we be happy with what we want to do....I guess Mrs. Anita is not going for a film rehearsal after learning from me". Mrs. Nayar looked up...her eyes trying to be thankful.....which was reciprocated by a very shabby nod from my side.

The virtual journey

So, I said....How do we practice....? My group members wanted it online as they found it more comfortable....besides..my friend could sit on the bed and do "dance practice"! Moreover...My simple and sublime Mita...has changed into a more smart and techie Mita. I adored this change in Mita...who lost her charm, was starting to look at her talents and nuances that mattered. I was feeling very happy because now Mita was developing a love for living life. And I was becoming happy to see that Mita with her back pain...was trying her best to beat the pain and trying to help herself...by being loving and accepting of her capabilities. She was turning out to be more sincere and intelligent....a lady who could now exactly define her problems and find new solutions that might have not been very important to others but mattered for her. In short...she was happy.

As I was a working lady, the group decided to have the practice on weekends. The time set was 4:15 PM. Least did I know that I was trying to make a world for these women that were filled with their unfulfilled desires, childhood dreams of dancing that perhaps could not be nurtured due to the environment, family, conventions, and later due to marriage and its following responsibilities. For me, it was good to know that every individual has some desires that go unheard but deep within it struggle to find a hand to take it forward, a voice that will allow it to speak, an activity that will allow being exhibited and an uproar that would force its way out only to be recognized and loved. It might not become a full-time job or a career...but what it will do will be giving some novelty to their otherwise monotonous schedule of cooking, cleaning, looking after the household. Since the time I have been growing up, I have heard that 'Change" is important and if you do not change...you tend to be "discarded". The change that these ladies were looking forward to was something that none of us knew!! It was only in the process that we came to know each other better by feeling how close we came to understand each other. What was wonderful was that through a folk dance....I was getting connected to people who did not know the language but because the latent desire got a push, they were slowly becoming happy in their little world...... Let me introduce to you my" battalion.......that started dancing within".

We met once....again in Mrs. Nayar's house. This time "we" was much smaller. It comprised of Mrs. Das, Mrs. Shah, my dear friend Mita, my neighbor from Madhya Pradesh, Rachita, and the lovely Mrs. Nayar, the mother of two grown-up daughters and a husband who believed in doing a lot of charity. Not finding much time for charity at home Mrs. Nayar...yearned for something that could keep her busy. My idea of having idli sambhar was replaced by hard fried samosa and soft drinks. I wish I could tell Mrs. Nayar of my longing desire to have dosas...but having some consideration for her feelings that might have shown themselves up due to Mrs. Shah's non - acceptable and judgemental comments, I took upon myself as the happiness leader of the group. Not that I knew how to do it...but what I knew was only respecting humanity and its thoughts in whatever form they may be....whether Mrs. Nayar... or Mrs. Shah. Not that I started taking a dislike towards Mrs. Shah...but I started feeling sad about how backward we are in our thoughts. Education in its evolving nature yet needs to do much more than what is expected!!

The "unshackling" group had at least ten to twelve members...but astonishingly not more than three or four were willing to participate in the dance activity. Strange to see...that we have grown up physiologically but a lot of time and effort is still required to move out of the traditional social baggage..that at times automatically may be responsible for our "not so much developing ideas". To maintain social acceptance and dignity.....some were very welcoming and said would watch us doing the moves. Mrs. Shah....with a rustic look and golden spectacles gave us a stare that I seemed to have in my maths class, coming from my Maths teacher. No wonder that I traveled years back...it had found a bridge that defines the rustic look and that was, not very welcoming words. Praising her daughter's dance activity and her efforts for her daughter...she said..." for dance, we need to have practice....I don't think you will look nice". With no one of us ready to compare ourselves with her daughter..started thinking about a song that was full of energy and color of love...that we hoped to ignite.

Nonetheless my friend Mita, mostly suffering due to chronic back pain..had the courage of looking at me and saying.." Do you think I can do it?" Of course, Mita had to gather a lot of courage for asking me this question. Simply put...she had the desire to do it ...and saw me as the medium of completing her desires but probably she did not have the mental agility and strength, to carry her wish forward.

Appreciating her courage to move forward with time... I looked at her...Her innocence was as pure as it could be, not deterred by Mrs. Shah's mockery, was an event that made me believe that I can make her believe in herself which she lost probably in the rigmarole of evolving life. With a pat on her shoulders that had ironed red color kurta and a colorful printed dupatta....I told her...."Yes off course Mita. Just try and come out of what you do regularly. Cooking, eating cleaning will not go away anywhere. They will always cling to you. So why not have some time to rejuvenate for next day's chores". Mita was glowing. Probably, no one ever asked her to leave the chores for some time and enjoy what she loves. Her eyes...shining with admiration and her lips trying hard to tear apart and show the piece of calcium but the fear within of not performing was keeping her expressions at bay. Feeling her expressions, I asked her "Mita...I am so happy that you have shown interest. Believe me, your enthusiasm will help you deal with back pain that you keep on complaining about. Once you know how to manage it smilingly, I think you will stop speaking about your pain...and start doing things that you love to do. To be precise...I think you will be much more functional." Mita's world consisted of a scientist husband and her loving two children...who were also happy that their mother is trying to do something new. Mita got rolling and she said to me..." you know I used to dance a lot in Rabindra sangeet songs in school. I am so happy that you have reignited those memories. I love to go back where I belonged."

Mrs. Shah....having the terror of her life..did not seem very pleased with our conversation. Mrs. Nayar, feeling the punch, also patted Mita. Mrs. Shah was destroyed. Having punched Mrs. Shah in the mind....Mrs. Das seemed to have come to her aid... She said ...." please see that we are not disturbed while you practice. The constant noise of instruments like the tabla and tanpura...disturbs us..my children, who are studying and working find it uncomfortable." With Mrs. Nayar being the victim of mockery in its very rude form, it seemed to me that the saree draped Mrs. Das was finding it difficult to see the love for learning in Mrs. Nayar. Of course, community discomfort needs to be kept in mind but the mockery could have had a very sublime way of reaching out to Mrs. Nayar...the occupier of the top floor where Mrs. Das lived. Mrs. Nayar...felt bad...and what was surprising to me was that very few could see the pain she was going through when she showed enthusiasm to do something new. Well...I understood myself to be the happiness leader not without any reason..what say?

What we have lost is a way of reciprocating our disgust....as the mind struggles ferociously between what we have got, what we have not got, and constantly comparing ourselves with others and the best and privileged outcome is the "blame game". Whatever wrong happens to us is because of others, not because at times we may fail to make some strategic moves. Little did Freud realize that the defense mechanisms that he profoundly spoke about in his psychoanalytic theory, which mainly protects the ego....has turned out to be a "survival tool to beat the selfish existence". Little did he realize that the theory though latently would have such a serious impact. Mrs. Nayar...moving to and fro in her red-colored sofa which surprisingly was a contrast and complementary to our dress colors, looked down...as if she was punished and said in a very melancholic voice..." so...Mrs. Roy...is there any place where we can practice, as Mrs. Das is not comfortable with us dancing to happiness."

Looking at her face...which was as humble as it could be, I said..."Oh...Mrs. Nayar....we can have the practice on the virtual platform. I hope Mrs. Das will be OK with it?' Mrs. Das playing with the corner of the saree sensed the sarcasm in my voice. She said...

"I did not mean that..what I meant was to dance slowly".

Listening to this sentence, which to me made no sense...I said...Mrs. Das, it is dancing and not walking! Well, for me a virtual platform will be OK." Inside I was struggling to keep my anger at bay. I was controlling myself so that I do not speak badly with Mrs. Das..as she was very much senior to me. My traditions and customs somehow were taking an upper hand even during these times of human shame.

Mrs. Das was quiet...My friend Mita...was overjoyed as she would love to stay at home and have some sleep before the practice classes. Mrs. Ghosh...discussing various shampoos that she has used to prevent hair fall said..." yes, that is fine...but keep it in the evenings." Little did I know that Mrs. Ghosh will not find it interesting in the future and will not join the platform. With her curly hair and beautiful dancing moves.....she seemed to have been worried about her son's evening snacks and how horrified she was to go back home and cook...for the son and husband.

Finding this as an absolute solution...I asked Mrs. Nayar... to give me some more names who could join the platform. The names she suggested, in her holy innocence...did not seem to be sincere or dedicating towards learning. Something that I prized...while doing any activity, be it cooking, studying, or learning anything new. To my excitement....I immediately proposed the name of Rachita...a lady from Madhya Pradesh, with two kids. Her son studied with my daughter. Rachita was simple...not knowing the harshness of humanity, was busy applying Henna to her falling hair. With growing greys...her desire to make them red demanded great physical dexterity...and ultimately to her astonishment resulted in punishment. She went to the parlor with a paste of henna. She was denied services because she made the paste at home and did not ask the parlor people to book an appointment for her, which meant more money for the Salon. Surprised with their behavior.. humanity becoming more like business and less empathetic...she applied it herself..once she returned home.

Rachita...a lady having done Ayurveda...had deepest desires to learn dancing...but as luck would have it...she could not do it. Asking her to be a part of this group made her more than happy. When Mrs. Nayar called her up from her home ...she was overjoyed, speaking in great surprise..little knowing that Mrs. Nayar was insulted for the same. But listening to her voice Mrs. Nayar's sad look changed into a composed form. She said.."Rachita is ready, she is overjoyed. So madam...let's start the virtual group this Saturday. You tell us the time. We will do as you please." With Mrs. Das and Mrs. Shah forced to look down, having mixed feelings of shame and anger, we started the procedure by waving goodbye. Having the deep-fried samosa...that had

SAMOSA

Not truly satisfied with samosa...if Mrs. Nayar could hear that!!!

lost its charm amidst the management activity...made it a bit difficult to sense the taste ...My taste buds were in connivance with the mind to have dosas...that found it difficult to settle down for samosa and a cold drink. Nonetheless....my taste buds were quick enough to adjust to the replacement. Having finished my plate...I bid goodbye to the group...putting back my shackles as I needed to go back home and make my daughter study for her upcoming exams. For unshackling, Mita, myself, and Rachita were required to wait for Saturday and Sunday.

So, while helping Mrs. Shah and Mrs. Das calm down by our so-called "new ways of thinking", we decided to do our practice every Saturday and Sunday at 4:15 PM. The four of us hardly knew that we were entering a world that recognizes effort, time, respect for one another, takes criticism positively, and above all, there will be immense love for each other. So every Saturday morning, I, my daughter, or my husband had the extra job of sending a wats app message confirming the dance class. My loving family appreciated my love for dance or rather my respect for these courageous women who are novices in the art came in front, to learn few steps. Not knowing the reason behind this or rather not being interested in this logical investigation, I was happy to see that I could see them laughing and giggling during the practice. With everyone not easy with the online platform...for me it was a medium of bringing up those memories that were dwelling deep in our skull!! As we grow up, we hardly take note of the good things we have done like reciting poems, making drawings, or even writing. We grow up with worries of the future that is not certain, and the constant worry has the function of ruining the present.

Keeping the conventional stereotype thoughts behind coming from neighbors, my battalion was ready for the go! To my surprise, Mita, Mrs. Anita Nayar, and Rachita were excited to do the dance moves, though the muscles and bones must have been in great shock! Mrs. Nayar's urge to learn made her a person who defeats her age and that too with grace...by learning something new. It was only in the dance class that we all came to know that she learns Karnataka music, the violin that itself was wonderful! With her muscles lacking flexibility and constantly asking her to correct her moves, Mrs. Nayar..had a smile that would give you the power to teach with precision and clarity. For a dance move...I took the liberty of telling her for one part of the song and the dance move related to that -

"Mrs. Nayar...the movement has to be like you are so happy because your soulmate is talking about you". Being the senior-most of our battalion...Mrs. Nayar laughed as if she has not laughed for ages! Her emotions rekindled...and the moves started becoming more polished. Cherishing our moments of love...the honesty of which can make us feel very powerful. I only hoped that Mrs. Shah and Mrs. Das could only see the benefits rather than carrying the shackles of conventions that sometimes become suffocating. Everybody started smiling....

Rachita with her funny croaking sound said....." Oh...Oh..Anita Ji (Ji is used for someone elder), you seem to be blushing".

Mita with her perfect smile said.."Rachita ...you also think of your soulmate...your, steps will also improve then." With a natural humane tendency of taking it as a mockery did not happen! Mita had a good intention of helping Rachita with her sleek figure but inflexible bone structure because of which she was having serious problems in doing the leg movement. Not quite getting there and jumping in an inarticulate form...Rachita took it very nicely. I had a battalion that was welcoming of positive criticism. Rachita with sparkling eyes and husk voice due to laughter said...." yes Mita...I think that would work." Mrs. Nayar...added to the smiling and laughter episode...quiet acknowledging her emotions and feelings. My battalion was growing with inner strength and power to perform. A group that had no idea of dance was doing dance steps...was learning the beats of music..was trying to understand every word of the song..was trying to sync motor and listening abilities that might be difficult for these novice dancers...!!

Slowly but lovingly, this group became a place where we would share our feelings, our problems, and our desires..that so far maybe could not find appreciative ears and sober simplicity. No one was judged...or rather we can say that the group was so simple and clean ...that judgment did not show up at least in the most infamous ways. Laughing and giggling with each other filled us with positive energy...eagerly waiting for the coming weekend. This dancing group was a treasure that showed me that good people are around...you just need to find them. How it happens is a matter of destiny....my craving for dosas....saw a fantastic beginning..something that I did not have any clue about.

With hands getting out of proportion ...in music...Mrs. Nayar...was asked to do a lot of freehand exercises. Little did she know that her otherwise submissive nature will be very much evident in her body language. Being a psychologist by profession, understanding body language was a part of our curriculum....never thought it will be applicable even in the happiest times. I could not gather the courage to ask Mrs. Nayar about her behavior and personality traits...but what I told her was this....

"Anita Ji...Open your hands wide..as if you are trying to fly."

During the dance activity, I asked all my lovely dancers to do some free hands along with Mrs. Nayar. Whether Mrs. Nayar..could understand my interpretation of her body moves or not... remains an unclear question...because suddenly...Anita Ji's hand movement showed improvement. I think highly of Mrs. Anita Nayar..not only because she was the senior-most but also because she did not know the Bengali language in which we were putting our hands together. Making her and Rachita understand the meaning of each word was in itself self consoling and self fancy.... Consoling because we all cherished our younger years of infatuation, love, and care. It was self-fancy because we forgot about our likes and dislikes....how we used to decorate ourselves...all in the process of evolving. Till now everything seems so real and close to the heart...which might have been hurt due to many unexpected life events. This group helped us to revive rejuvenate...and appreciate.

My friend Mita was no exception...from this...Being a very solemn person in her genuine entirety, she passively started understanding the nuances of human behavior. She now started talking about many things that would reveal how simple my friend was in this world...that at times disregards simplicity. Practicing..dance every day...made my friend....forget about her pain in the back. I was so happy to see her practice videos. She was blooming. Her husband said to me while buying vegetables in the market and bumped into me...

"Hello, how are you?"

I am fine Mr. Chatterjee....how about you...?

He replied with a grumpy face..." trying to be happy while I am at home...my wife makes me run errands if I am sitting idle at home."

I replied with a consoling voice 'your wife seems to be dancing pretty well".

He replied with a somewhat appreciative tone..." You have kept her busy...good going Mrs. Roy".

Ready for dance class next Saturday.....Mita was always overjoyed. She felt she was out of a cage where a different world is waiting. Not that she was in a dire state....only that she had till date not known the process of unshackling. She had not known how to cherish what she has. For me, she had good observational, understanding, and imitating skills. If it was not for the dance class, then my battalion wouldn't have known the skill of writing poems that Mita had. Mita now had a channel. What Mita required was a world that would make her feel empowered in whatever way it was possible. The dance classes had a wonderful effect. She entered a world of pure humanity. A world that has no judgment, no malice except for the love of each other's ability. I had not known Saturdays and Sundays will give me so much happiness....other than being relieved from official work. My battalion was a bunch of talent that just needed some grooming.

With my friends waiting eagerly for 4:15, where meeting other people was just a click away, my friends Rachita and Anita Ji...seemed to be more enthusiastic about evolving. Considering Mrs. Nayar's belief in her abilities after she became very ill and was dependent upon medicines to survive, she regained her strength and started looking for all possibilities that could make her happy. Managing the household chores and looking after two small children Rachita and Mrs. Nayar..found some time every day in the morning to practice. Good to know that they were enjoying themselves. Though we had some members who showed reluctance in the beginning...we somehow through our dedication and love for learning made these ladies join our dance class. Not knowing whether it was for motivation, or something else but our unshackling was doing the rounds!

With the ending of the dance practice approaching....I decided to upload a video about women opening up. So I asked them

The youtube video of the battalion...

"Hey....I would like to make a video of our dance. We have worked so hard...so our friends and family should see". Mita answered in a tone quite unlikely of her personality!! With a smile that shows humbleness and purity...her eyes...sparkling as if they could see the stars that they have wanted to see so far...said..." oh wow....but how will it happen?" Rachita on the other hand was curious to know about the dress and jewelry she would use to decorate herself. Mrs. Nayar...was happy to accommodate with the traditional folk dance culture....but it was a mere pleasure to be discussing the saree she was required to wear, the hairstyle of the folk dancers, and the jewelry. It was some paper jewelry that counselor we were trying to settle down for that had a silver.....metallic look. All of them were excited. Rachita...with all her excitement brought in front of the camera hair clip that had yellow flowers on it. She had purchased it for a marriage party that she was deciding to attend. The physical dexterity saw leaps and bounds with everyone sharing their jewelry and ideas in front of the camera. It looked like a mini "Meena bazaar".

So ..apart from the dancing classes that we had every weekend....was seeing a transformation into an online boutique....where we were showcasing the sarees that we wanted to wear for the video. Everyone opened their hearts out to a situation that demanded virtual ways of survival. Dancing is my passion and not a profession..was the only way that was making me pass through a time that needed much more physical, emotional, and mental strength.

Mrs. Nayar..came with a white and red border saree, peculiar to Bengali culture..and asked...At last Mrs. Nayar..seeing her children grow and having their own space, was open enough to create her own space. She now wanted to be a child "Anita" who wanted to do everything she could. Giving her full strength to the family, she now took to love herself and live her dreams. With her dream of looking beautiful as a child, in a regressive voice, she asked me...

"Which one will look good on me?" We all said...".the white one....".Mrs. Nayar..ran into her room to get her bangles. Rachita also showed her saree....Rachita was a different person now...or maybe I was getting to know her more!!! She was sincere and obedient. Finding it difficult to dress up like a folk dancer....Rachita took all the effort to look like one. My battalion quite matched with the one that we were dancing to..... We were all flying to our happiness in the sky. My battalion was now becoming more powerful. By "powerful" I don't mean a show of physical greatness but what I meant was that they were growing in their thinking, in their emotional management. My friend Mita who preferred doing the class while sitting on the bed had a love for "make-up. It became a well-known fact when we were discussing how we should decorate our faces. Mita while practicing in the bed said

"I love to do make-up, but the fact is I do not look good with make-up".

After being surprised with Mita's love for make-up, which made every one of us raise our eyebrows...I said ...." Mita don't worry.....you will look pretty...after all, you have such a pretty heart".

Finally after much effort and rehearsals ...our video was being made....I was delighted...with no clue where the dance class would stand....I was happy to see that it not only became a wonderful piece of humanity and growth...but also was quite a revelation itself. The dance class lead to hope that was ignited, There was color and love in every action that we did. My battalion had conquered their own "SELVES". They now knew what they really wanted and how to take care of their desires. They were indeed dancing within.

Mita as an extension of herself and realizing her potentials now is learning the flute. Mrs. Nayar is living the dreams of her life by learning more dancing steps from me and Rachita...in the due course has become a dear friend who loves to learn, unlearn and relearn.

Women unshackling has broken the shackles of self-suffering. It has made us walk through our dreams by being loving, accepting, and compassionate of the true selves that have been evolving without much attention from us. But now ...we know how important it is to look out for our true selves.

A small poem...written for my Battalion....
" Myself and Thyself

Know not what lies ahead
What is in store
I wish I could know more
Idlis, chicken, curry, dal and sabzi
With house and cleanliness
No more remain my only chore
As I have learned to grow
To give love by being loved
For what I have lost
That remains in the wilderness
No one knows my skills
Except in the art of household management
Looking for a Chance
That could take me out of the shore
By flapping wings, whose color now unfold
When I look within
Helps me see myself dancing, singing, creating
A woman that has layers of wisdom
A woman whose chore now evolves from collaboration
to compassion
For unknown and quiet victories ahead
Hope is now ignited
Colors are everywhere
Love remains in our hearts and actions
With a subtle change
That brings even more love for myself and my close
ones.

Enter Caption